OnBoard
ACADEMICS

Context

© 2015 OnBoard Academics, Inc
Portsmouth, NH
800-596-3175
www.onboardacademics.com
ISBN: 978-1-63096-043-8

OnBoard Academic's books are specifically designed to be used as printed workbooks or as on-screen instruction. Each page offers focused exercises and students quickly master topics with enough proficiency to move on to the next level.

OnBoard Academic's lessons are used in over 25,000 classrooms to rave reviews. Our lessons are aligned to the most recent governmental standards and are updated from time to time as standards change. Correlation documents are located on our website. Our lessons are created, edited and evaluated by educators to ensure top quality and real life success.

Interactive lessons for digital whiteboards, mobile devices, and PCs are available at www.onboardacademics.com. These interactive lessons make great additions to our books.

You can always reach us at customerservice@onboardacademics.com.

Summarize and Paraphrase

Key Vocabulary

summarize

paraphrase

plagiarize

Definitions

Find the correct match for each definition

☐ Restate a passage or an idea in your own words.

☐ Use sentences or phrases taken directly from a passage.

☐ State the main idea and key points in a passage.

S ummarize   **P** araphrase   **Q** uote

Whether you are summarizing, paraphrasing, or quoting, if you include an author's work in your own work, the original source should *always* be attributed.

Messages in Bottles by Rebecca Livermore

What can be more intriguing than a message in a bottle? If you put a message in a bottle, and tossed it into the ocean, what are the odds that someone would find it, where would it end up, and how long would it take? And who in the world first came up with the idea of putting a message in a bottle anyway?

These are some the questions that may have came to the mind of Merle Brandell, an Alaskan beachcomber who found a bottle that had been launched by a fourth grade student, Emily Hwaung, in 1986. The bottle took approximately 21 years to travel 1,735 miles from Seattle to Alaska!

The ancient Greek philosopher Theophrastus is the first person known to have released a message in a bottle around 310 BC. He wanted to show that the Mediterranean Sea is formed by the inflowing Atlantic Ocean. Christopher Columbus was another historical message-in-abottler. Caught up in a severe storm at sea, he placed a report of his discoveries in a bottle along with a note asking that it be passed on to the Queen of Spain. He hoped that his report might be received even if he did not survive the storm. In the event, Columbus did survive, but to this day, no one knows what became of his message in a bottle.

Although we usually think of discovering a message in a bottle as an exciting event, in the 16th century, reading a message in a bottle could result in very severe penalties. This is because the English navy used messages in bottles to send secret information about enemy positions and other intelligence reports. After finding out that a boatman at Dover had accidentally opened one of these secret messages, Queen Elizabeth created a new job position: *Uncorker of Ocean Bottles.* Henceforth, the official *Uncorker of Ocean Bottles* was the only person permitted to open found bottles. Unauthorized uncorkers would be put to death.

Of course, a message in a bottle is best known as the communication of last resort for people who are shipwrecked or lost at sea. And it can be a successful strategy. In May of 2005, a large group of migrants who had been shipwrecked off the coast of Costa Rica sent out a cry for help in a message in a bottle which they tied to a long line on a passing fishing boat. Their bottle was found and they were rescued.

Others lost souls have not had such a fortunate ending. In 1748, Japanese seaman, Chunosuke Matsuyama, who was shipwrecked along with 44 of his mates, carved a message on a piece of wood and placed it in a bottle. Unfortunately, it was not found until 150 years later.

Messages in bottles have been an enduring form of communication on the ocean because glass bottles are very seaworthy. They do not sink, and can bob around for seemingly endless periods of time without being damaged. However, if you do ever find yourself lost at sea, while it won't hurt to put a message in a bottle and pray for the best, the odds of it leading to your rescue are slim. This is because it's impossible to predict where a message in a bottle will end up or how long it will take to get there. The speed at which a bottle travels is dependent on wind and current and many other variables. As proof of this uncertainty, consider the passage of two bottles which were dropped at the same time in the same place off the coast of Brazil. One bottle made its way east and after 130 days was found on a beach in Africa. The other bottle was at sea for 190 days and disembarked in Nicaragua!

Summarize, Paraphrase or Quotation?

☐ Rebecca Livermore says that messages in bottles are an unreliable way to communicate because "... it's impossible to predict where a message in a bottle will end up, or how long it will take to get there."

☐ The author describes how messages in bottles have been used throughout history, particularly by people who are lost at sea. She points out that it's a very unreliable way to communicate, though, because the bottles travel in a very unpredictable manner.

☐ In her article on messages in bottles, Rebecca Livermore describes how Christopher Columbus placed a report of his discoveries in a bottle just in case he didn't survive a violent storm at sea.

S ummary   **P** araphrase   **Q** uotation

The writer attempted to paraphrase paragraph four.

Reread paragraph four of "Messages in a Bottle" and then read the writer's attempt to paraphrase. The writer had a problem on each attempt and the problem is highlighted in red.

1 In the 16th century a special job role called the *Uncorker of Ocean Bottles* was created so that secret military communications would not be read by ordinary citizens. Anyone else who opened an ocean bottle would be executed.
The source is not attributed.

2 In her article on messages in bottles, Rebecca Livermore describes how in the 16th century, because a boatman opened a secret message in a bottle from the English navy, the Queen created a new job role called the *Uncorker of Ocean Bottles.* This person was the only one permitted to open found bottles. Anyone else would be put to death.
Too close to original source (plagiarization).

3 In her article on messages in bottles, Rebecca Livermore describes how in the 16th century a special job role called the *Uncorker of Ocean Bottles* was created.
Key facts are missing.

Now it's your turn to paraphrase paragraph four.

_____

_____

_____

_____

_____

_____

_____

_____

The King Cobra by Shelly Barclay

King Cobras are the largest venomous snakes on Earth. Found in the forests and grasslands of Southeast Asia, they can be recognized by the telltale hood that spreads out behind their head when threatened. This hood is actually a set of ribs that can be stretched out to give the King Cobra its distinctive and formidable appearance.

An adult King Cobra is usually about twelve feet long and weighs around thirteen pounds. Larger specimens have been recorded, but are rare. They are tan, olive green or black in color, and have yellow bands along the entire length of their bodies, with a light, yellowish underside. Able swimmers and climbers, they have an average lifespan of 20 years. Adult King Cobras shed their skin up to five times a year, while adolescents shed as much as once a month.

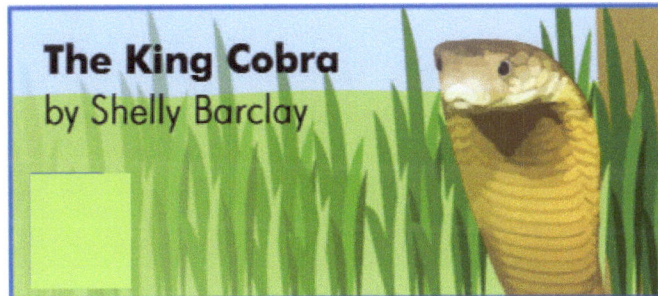

King Cobras subsist mainly on a diet of other snakes. They can go for months at a time without eating, but when pressed for food, they will also eat lizards, rodents and birds. They hunt using their unique sense of smell and by interpreting vibrations, and like all other snakes, they have hinged jaws that enable them to eat their prey by swallowing it whole.

Female King Cobras lay clutches of 20-40 eggs in nests of leaves, and these eggs incubate for roughly three months. The mother then abandons the nest as soon as her young start hatching. She does this instinctively so that she will not be tempted to eat them.

King Cobras are, of course, notoriously dangerous. A single King Cobra bite in the right place is sufficient to kill an adult elephant, while the generally accepted human mortality rate for

King Cobra bites is as high as 75%. The venom of a King Cobra is *neurotoxic*, which means that it attacks the central nervous system. Its venom is actually less potent than that of some other dangerous snake species, but due to its large size, the King Cobra produces more venom per bite, which is why it is the most lethal.

People unfortunate enough to be bitten by a King Cobras often experience a myriad of symptoms including blurry vision, severe pain, cardiovascular complications, and vertigo. Other symptoms like necrosis may arise if the victim survives long enough, although respiratory failure is usually the ultimate cause of death. As antivenin is not always readily available, avoidance is by far the best defense against a King Cobra bite.

Write a one paragraph summary of "The King Cobra" and then compare it to the summary on the next page.

_____

_____

_____

_____

_____

_____

_____

_____

_____

_____

_____

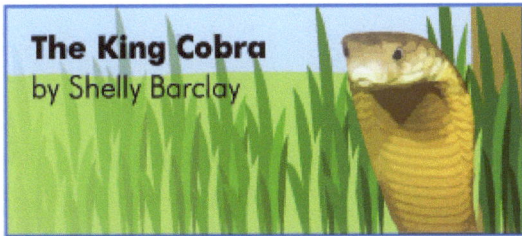

The King Cobra
by Shelly Barclay

In her article on King Cobras, Shelly Barclay describes the habitat, appearance, and diet of these fascinating, but deadly creatures. At an average length of about 12 feet, the King Cobra is the world's biggest poisonous snake, and so lethal that, according to this article, 3 out of every 4 people who are bitten by a King Cobra do not survive. The King Cobra's hood, which gives the snake "its distinctive and formidable appearance," is a sign that the snake feels threatened. Due to its toxicity and the lack of antivenins, Barclay recommends that you give the King Cobra a very wide berth.

Can you name some points that the author of this summary covered that you did not?

What is different about your summary when compared to this one?

Here is a writer's attempt to paraphrase paragraph five of "The King Cobra."

Comment on each attempt to paraphrase the paragraph.

According to Shelly Barclay, in her article on King Cobras, about half of the people who are bitten by a King Cobra will die. This is because the King Cobra is the most venomous snake in the world.

Comment

According to Shelly Barclay, in her article on King Cobras, a single King Cobra bite can kill an adult elephant. For humans, the mortality rate is about 75%. This is not because the King Cobra is the most venomous snake in the world though. It is due to its large size. That's why it's so lethal.

Comment

In her article on King Cobras, author Shelly Barclay points out that although the King Cobra is not the most venomous snake in the world, it is the most lethal because it is such a big snake and injects so much venom. Barclay says that about 3 out of every 4 people who are bitten by a King Cobra will die.

Comment

Name_____

Summarize and Paraphrase Quiz

1. A quote must be attributed, but a paraphrase uses your
   own words so attribution isn't needed. True or false?

2. What is plagiarizing?
   a. paraphrasing
   b. copying
   c. quoting
   d. summarizing

3. Which of the following must be included in a direct
   quote?
   a. your own words
   b. quotation marks
   c. your own name
   d. all of the above

4. A book reports contains paraphrases of the main ideas
   in a book. True or false?

5. Which of the following is the best definition of a
   summary?
   a. Restatement of the facts in the correct order.
   b. Restatement of the main idea and the key facts.
   c. Restatement of the text in your own words.
   d. None of the above.

Fact vs. Opinion

Key Vocabulary

fact

opinion

Fact vs. Opinion

Apples are low in calories and free of fat.

I think apples are the most delicious fruit.

_____

Apples are low in calories and free of fat.

I think apples are the most delicious fruit.

A **fact** is a statement based on direct evidence and can be *proven to be true.*

An **opinion** is a statement of belief or feeling and is someone's *viewpoint.*

Sorting Fact vs. Opinion

Sort the sentences below.

fact	opinion

I am the best at Sudoku.

$4{,}125 \times 120 = 495{,}000$

James has the coolest dog.

Science is a boring subject.

Bill Clinton was President.

It was 73 degrees yesterday.

Red is the best color!

Mia is doing laundry today.

Identify if the sentence is a fact (F) or if the sentence is an opinion (O).

1 Spiders are scary. ☐

2 Oil is less dense than water. ☐

3 Brussel sprouts are disgusting. ☐

4 Spiders have eight legs. ☐

5 You are very mean. ☐

6 Augusta is the capital of Maine. ☐

Fact or Opinion Clues

> **Certain words often let you know if a statement is an *opinion*. Among these are *best, worst, most, least, should, good,* and *bad*.**

_____

Label the each text as either fact or opinion.

fact

opinion

	I bought the best phone yesterday
	Oh, you must've gone to the new electronics store that just opened.
	Yes, they had a grand opening sale so my mom took me.
	My sister just got a new phone too.
	Mine is a very pretty red color.

Circle the facts and underline the opinions.

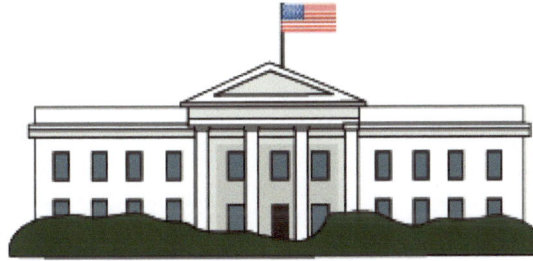

The American President has the best job in the world. He lives in the White House at 1600 Pennsylvania Ave., Washington D.C. The mansion has 132 rooms, 28 fireplaces, and the most amazing view of the city. It also has five full-time chefs, tennis courts, and even a doctor's office! The President has the best amenities right at his fingertips without ever leaving home.

Circle facts and underline opinions in this article.

FRIDAY, SEPTEMBER 15   US $2.50

The Eagle Daily Press

Super Senior Strikes Spectacular Shot!

110-year-old golfer, Bert Hacker, yesterday became the oldest person ever to shoot a hole in one. This incredible feat occurred at the exclusive Baloney Bay Golf and Country Club. Bert's ace, his first ever, was at the final hole on the course, a par 3 with a beautiful view overlooking Baloney Bay.

Bert's golf partner, Fred 'Shank' Shipton, described the event. "Bert hit a great shot," said Shipton, "and I knew it was going in the hole." Baloney Bay Golf Pro, Dave Pringle, said that no-one would ever match Bert's accomplishment. "It's a once-in-a-lifetime achievement," said Pringle. "Most people of Bert's age would prefer to be at home dozing," he said.

Bert himself was very modest about his achievement "It was a complete fluke!" he said.

Sometimes news articles or programs can mix fact and opinion. It is important to question whether something is based on verifiable information or someone's particular viewpoint.

Name_____

Fact vs. Opinion Quiz

1. An opinion can often be disguised as a fact in a news article. True or false?

2. Which of the following is a fact?
   a. Everyone hates rain.
   b. Snow is better than rain.
   c. Science is boring
   d. Drops of water form clouds

3. Channel 3 News reported that the new shopping mall which opened today on Seventh Street will be a nice addition to the neighborhood.
   a. fact
   b. opinion

4. Which of the following is a fact?
   a. Insects are creepy.
   b. Spiders are not good pets.
   c. Ladybugs are cute.
   d. Ants are insects.

5. Chocolate ship cookies are the tastiest.
   a. fact
   b. opinion

Context Clues

Key Vocabulary

context clue(s)

subject

predicate

context

Context Clues

Find a word to replace the word procured in the sentence that is supported by the clues.

Principal Garcia
has procured 20 new laptops.

■ subject
■ predicate

Is the word in the subject?
Am I looking for a noun?

Is the word in the predicate?
Am I looking for a verb?

Use What You Know

Use what you know about a sentence to find the meaning of an unknown word.

> **The word is in the predicate and is a verb.**
>
> **Mrs. Garcia is the principal, and the laptops are new.**

_____

Find a word to replace the word procured in the sentence that is supported by the clues.

Principal Garcia has procured **20 new laptops.**

- ○ polished
- ○ high-speed
- ○ purchased
- ○ repaired

Practice using what you know to find the meaning of an unknown word.

A **proponent** of the new road said that it would help to reduce traffic jams.

○ critic

○ drives

○ brakes

○ supporter

Subject or predicate?
Would reducing traffic jams
be a good or bad thing?

_____

Find a word to replace the word procured in the sentence that is supported by the clues.

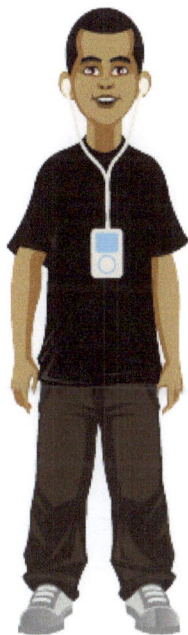

I already own great headphones, and so the cheap ones that came with the MP3 player are **superfluous** .

○ tangled

○ unnecessary

○ downloads

○ mine

Context Clue Crossword Puzzle

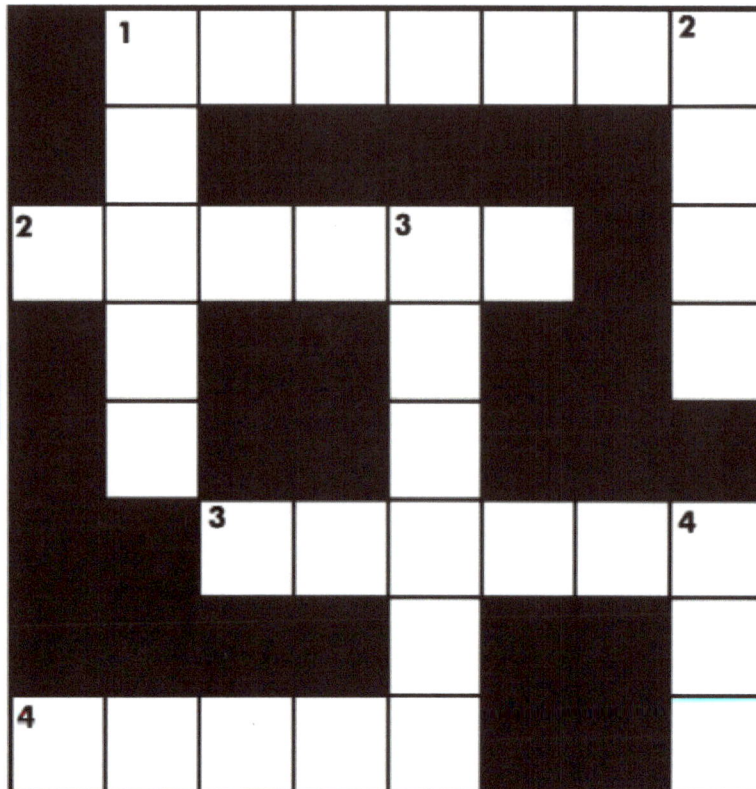

ACROSS

1. Victory was **ASSURED** when Gomez scored his third goal.

2. They were good neighbors and so discussions about the new fence were very **CORDIAL**.

3. The abandoned house had become very **UNKEMPT**.

4. They had insufficient **CAPITAL** for the deposit on the house.

DOWN

1. The blowout sale attracted a **THRONG** of people to the mall.

2. His **PROBOSCIS** was red due to a very bad cold.

3. A **COVENANT** was signed that would end the war.

4. "Are you receiving me?" "**AFFIRMATIVE**. I can hear you loud and clear!"

Name_____

Context Clues Quiz

1. James finished his homework promptly so that he could play with his friends.
   a. quickly
   b. slowly
   c. carefully
   d. happily

2. "Submit your own work," said the teacher. "Do not plagiarize the work of others."
   a. submit
   b. design
   c. copy
   d. homework

3. The workout in the hot gym made Amy perspire.
   a. run
   b. Grumpy
   c. fit
   d. sweat

4. The poison ivy caused her to have a rash on her epidermis. Where is the rash?
   a. shoe
   b. skin
   c. hair
   d. shirt

Cause and Effect

Key Vocabulary

cause

effect

Cause and Effect

To determine which event is the cause and which is the effect, think about which event happens first. The cause always *happens* first. This doesn't mean that it always comes first in a sentence, e.g. "I don't have healthy teeth because I never brush or floss."

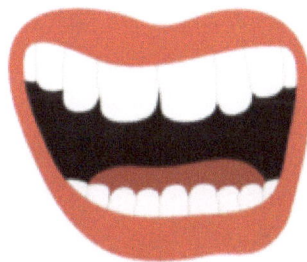

cause   If you don't brush and floss,

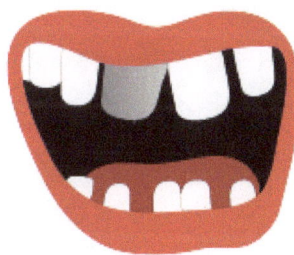

cause   If you don't brush and floss,
effect   you won't have healthy teeth.

Sort the cause and effect for each sentence.

Now circle the signal words as described below.

cause	effect

Since it was cold outside we wore hats and gloves.

Jenna's hat blew off because it was windy.

It snowed overnight so we built a snowman

As a result of the rain the game was cancelled.

> **Often, cause and effect relationships are "signaled" by words and phrases such as since, because, so, and as a result of.**
> **Can you think of any other signal words?**

> **Some additional "signal" words or phrases include therefore, and that's why, and due to.**

Circle causes and underline effects.

Escape from the Giant's Castle by Mia Lewis

We planned our escape at midnight because we knew the giant would be sleeping soundly. The lock on our cell door was rusty, so we were able to open it easily, but as we tiptoed quietly down the stone stairway, Alison accidentally stepped on the giant's sleeping cat, and it shrieked loudly. The sound woke the giant, and he came thundering down the stairs. But it was too late. The giant could not cross the moat until sunrise, and so we knew we were free!

www.onboardacademics.com

Effects can be both positive and negative.

My eldest brother got his license, so Mom let him borrow her car.

He was talking on his cell phc and crashed her car into a tre

Underline the effect and decide if it is positive or negative by adding a + or a - to the box.

My mom got a promotion at work,
so Dad took her out to dinner to celebrate.

They couldn't eat at her favorite restaurant
because they hadn't made a booking.

As it was a special occasion, Dad suggested
they try a new upscale French restaurant.

When the check came, Dad nearly fainted!

Name_____

Cause and Effect Quiz

1. The cause is the event that happens first. True or false?

2. If the cause is, I rode my bike quickly, wha tis the moste likely effect?
   a. I am a skillful bike rider.
   b. I tripped when I crossed the street.
   c. I was out of breath.
   d. I am the best.

3. If the effect is, I broke my ankle, what is the most likely cause?
   a. I made cookies
   b. I fell off my bike.
   c. I tied my shoe.
   d. I need crutches.

4. If the effect is, Xavier put in earplugs, what is the least likely cause?
   a. Xavier is going swimming.
   b. Xavier is going to a rock concert.
   c. Xavier is traveling by plane
   d. It's cold outside.

Compare and Contrast

Key Vocabulary

compare

contrast

Compare and contrast Nancy and Karen.

> **Compare** means to find the ways that things are *alike*.
> **Contrast** means to find the ways that things are *different*.

Circle the similarities and underline the differences.

Although Nancy and Karen are identical twins, people who know them can tell them apart quite easily. Nancy is very shy and quiet, while Karen is loud and outgoing. They are both good students, but they have different strengths. Nancy is good at math, while Karen is good at English. Nancy loves music and plays the violin. Karen loves music too, but her real passion is sports. Nancy thinks sports are a complete waste of time.

Organize information with a table or a t-chart.

Although Nancy and Karen are identical twins, people who know them can tell them apart quite easily. Nancy is very shy and quiet, while Karen is loud and outgoing. They are both good students, but they have different strengths. Nancy is good at math, while Karen is good at English. Nancy loves music and plays the violin. Karen loves music too, but her real passion is sports. Nancy thinks sports are a complete waste of time.

Nancy	Karen

likes music   good at math   shy and quiet

loves sports   likes music   looks like her sister

good student   looks like her sister   good student

good at English   loud and outgoing   hates sports

Venn Diagram

You can also organize information in a Venn Diagram.

Circle the area that contains similarities.

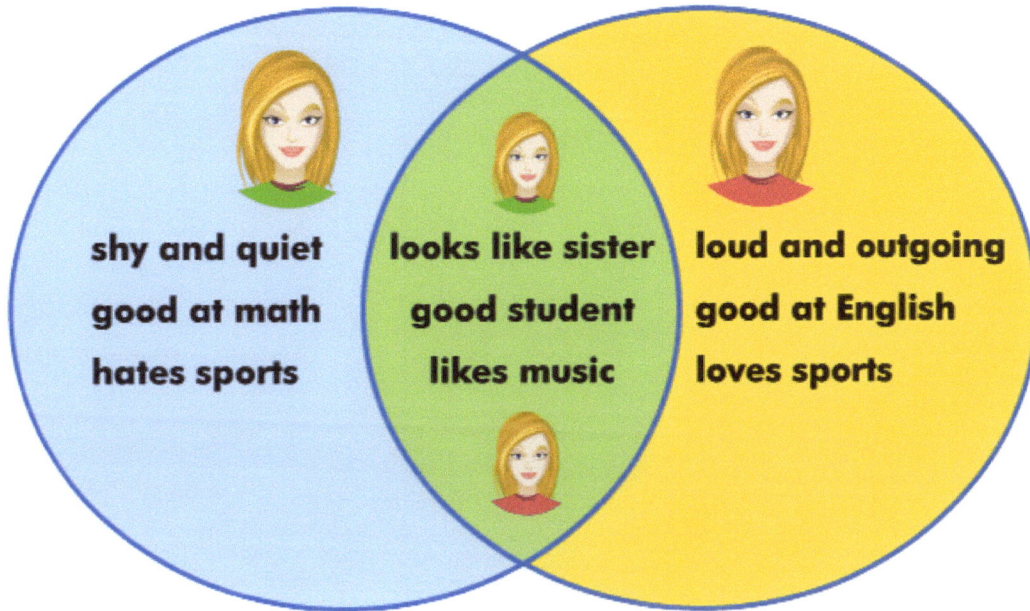

Compare and contrast these laptops.

Use whatever data organization tool you wish.

Great Gadgets Magazine reviews the e-Plus and the i-Power laptops.

Both of these laptops are stylish and well-built **too**. At $499, the e-Plus just has the edge on price, **but** the i-Power offers more features, including a larger screen and a faster DVD drive. **However**, the e-Plus makes up for this with a longer battery life. If you travel, the good news is that the e-Plus weighs just 4½ lb. The i-Power comes in at less than 5 lb **as well**, and **each** comes with a rugged carry case. Built-in wireless is standard on **both** models, **although** our editors did find it quite difficult to setup the wireless connection on the e-Plus.

Editors' overall rating

e-Plus ★★★★★

i-Power ★★★★☆

One way that the two laptops are alike is that they both:

○ include a carry case

○ cost less than $500

○ have large screens

○ weigh 4½ lb

Great Gadgets Magazine reviews the e-Plus and the i-Power laptops.

Both of these laptops are stylish and well-built **too**. At $499, the e-Plus just has the edge on price, **but** the i-Power offers more features, including a larger screen and a faster DVD drive. **However**, the e-Plus makes up for this with a longer battery life. If you travel, the good news is that the e-Plus weighs just 4½ lb. The i-Power comes in at less than 5 lb **as well**, and **each** comes with a rugged carry case. Built-in wireless is standard on **both** models, **although** our editors did find it quite difficult to setup the wireless connection on the e-Plus.

Editors' overall rating

e-Plus ★★★★★

i-Power ★★★★☆

One way that the two laptops are different is:

○ the e-Plus has a better case

○ the e-Plus doesn't have wireless

○ the e-Plus is cheaper

○ the e-Plus has a faster DVD

More Laptop Compare and Contrast

Great Gadgets Magazine reviews the e-Plus and the i-Power laptops.
Both of these laptops are stylish and well-built **too**. At $499, the e-Plus just has the edge on price, **but** the i-Power offers more features, including a larger screen and a faster DVD drive. **However**, the e-Plus makes up for this with a longer battery life. If you travel, the good news is that the e-Plus weighs just 4½ lb. The i-Power comes in at less than 5 lb **as well**, and **each** comes with a rugged carry case. Built-in wireless is standard on **both** models, **although** our editors did find it quite difficult to setup the wireless connection on the e-Plus.

Editors' overall rating
e-Plus ★★★★★
i-Power ★★★★☆

Another way that the two laptops are different is:

○ the e-Power has a better case

○ the e-Plus is easier to setup

○ the i-Power is better if you travel

○ the i-Power has more features

Great Gadgets Magazine reviews the e-Plus and the i-Power laptops.
Both of these laptops are stylish and well-built **too**. At $499, the e-Plus just has the edge on price, **but** the i-Power offers more features, including a larger screen and a faster DVD drive. **However**, the e-Plus makes up for this with a longer battery life. If you travel, the good news is that the e-Plus weighs just 4½ lb. The i-Power comes in at less than 5 lb **as well**, and **each** comes with a rugged carry case. Built-in wireless is standard on **both** models, **although** our editors did find it quite difficult to setup the wireless connection on the e-Plus.

Editors' overall rating
e-Plus ★★★★★
i-Power ★★★★☆

Another way that the two laptops are similar is that both:

○ have a good warranty

○ are easy to use and setup

○ cost less than $500

○ achieved at least a 4-star rating

Signal Words

Which signal words suggest a comparison (write them in the blue boxes) and which suggest a contrast (write them in the yellow boxes).

Crocodiles and Alligators

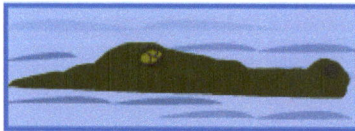

Crocodiles and alligators are **alike** in that **each** are crocodilians. That is the term given to large, lizard-shaped reptiles. Although they are in some ways quite **similar**, there are, **however**, several important **differences** between them. If you observe a crocodile when its mouth is closed, one of its lower teeth sticks up over its upper lip, **but** no teeth are visible on the closed mouth of an alligator. You'll also notice that the crocodile's snout is v-shaped. Alligators, **on the other hand**, have rounder more u-shaped snouts. Habitat is another good way to **separate** them. Alligators typically live in freshwater. Crocodiles live in freshwater, **too**, but prefer saltwater habitats. In **both** species, the male grows to be larger than the female.

Compare and contrast the USA and the UK.

Use a table to organize your information.

The US and the UK are alike in many ways. Both countries have large economies, both are democracies, we share many place names, and, of course, we share a common language too.

However, despite our common links and close ties to the UK, we are different in many ways. For one thing, the UK is a constitutional monarchy. This means that its official head of state is a queen or king. The US is also a much bigger place than the UK. About 40 times bigger in fact, with a population about five times that of the UK.

Teenagers in both countries share many of the same interests such as music, fashion, and computers, but our favorite sporting pastimes are different. In the UK, the major sports are soccer, cricket and rugby, while here in the US, it's football, baseball, basketball, and hockey... although many would argue that soccer (called *football* in the UK) is now a shared passion.

And even our common language can be quite different. We spell many words differently, and the same words sometimes have different meanings. For example, if you want to rent an apartment to someone from the UK, you should let them know that you have a "flat" to rent!

Name_____

Compare and Contrast Quiz

1. When you contrast two things, you describe the ways in which they are alike. True or false?

2. Which sentences compares sight and sound?
   a. Spectacles can help to improve your sight, but won't do anything for your hearing.
   b. Sight is related to seeing, while sound is related to hearing.
   c. Sight and sound are both senses.
   d. You use your ears for sound and your eyes for sight.

3. Which sentence contrasts juice and soda?
   a. Juice and soda are both good drinks on a hot day.
   b. There are many different types of juice and soda.
   c. Most people keep juice and soda in the fridge.
   d. Juice is a healthier drink than soda.

4. Which are signal words for contrast?
   a. both, too
   b. and, but
   c. too, while
   d. while, however

5. Which can be used to compare and contrast?
   a. Table
   b. T-Chart
   c. Venn diagram
   d. all of the above

Making Inferences

Key Vocabulary

infer

inference

imply

reasonable conclusion

context clue

antonym

synonym

www.onboardacademics.com

Inference

If you saw this picture and heard screeching tires and glass shatter what would you suppose would have happened?

_____

_____

_____

You've just made an **inference.** An inference is a **logical conclusion** based upon certain facts or evidence that you think support that logical conclusion.

A Quiet Word with Bruiser Barnes.

Jimmy was just on his way to math club when the hulking figure of Bruiser Barnes appeared around the corner.

"Hey, Kennedy!" shouted Barnes, "I need a quiet word with you!"

Jimmy swallowed hard and his knees began to tremble. If Bruiser Barnes wanted "a quiet word" with you, that could only mean one thing. As Barnes pounded toward him, Jimmy removed his glasses in preparation for what was to come, and he tried to imagine how the loss of some of his teeth might affect his relationship with Tori.

_____

Place a √ next to the conclusions can you reasonably infer from this passage.

①	Bruiser Barnes is a big guy.	
②	Jimmy likes math.	
③	Bruiser doesn't like "math geeks".	
④	Jimmy is nervous and anticipates violence.	
⑤	Bruiser might back off if confronted.	
⑥	Jimmy is dating Tori.	
⑦	Jimmy's friends from math club won't help him.	
⑧	Tori will dump Jimmy if he loses any teeth.	
⑨	The setting for the story is a school.	

Now read the end of A Quiet Word with Bruiser Barnes

Before Jimmy could reach the safety of the math club classroom, Bruiser was upon him.

"Uh, listen, Bruiser, " stuttered Jimmy. "My teeth are very fragile, and, I, uh, I mean, it's Tori, and, I, she, uh... "

Barnes looked confused.

"Listen, Kennedy," said Bruiser. "I'm not here to talk about your teeth. I wanted a quiet word with you as I'm thinking about joining the math club."

You can infer and make logical conclusions even if those conclusions prove to be inaccurate. Remember that an inference isn't a fact, it's a logical conclusion based upon evidence that you think supports that logical conclusion.

Context Clues

Use context clues help infer meanings of unknown words.

Ernie is very [**garrulous**]. This gets him in trouble at school as his teacher is always telling him to stop chattering in class. His dad calls him "motor mouth," and he has even been banned from his local library.

Circle the definition of garrulous.

naughty   talkative   disruptive

_____

Circle the definition of prevaricate.

"Please don't [prevaricate], Grace," said her mother. "There are cookie crumbs all over your bed and so there's no point claiming that you didn't take them. Why don't you just admit it?"

laugh   lie   shout

Using Antonyms to Infer Meaning

Owen is very outgoing and confident, but his brother Ben is quite diffident .

tall   shy   spunky

_____

Imply vs. Infer

Learn the difference.

To **imply** is to put a suggestion *into* the message or text, while to **infer** is to to take a suggestion *out of the* message or text.

www.onboardacademics.com

Name_____

Making Inferences Quiz

1. If David pulls a face when he eats an anchovy, he is implying that he doesn't like anchovies. True or false?

2. What can you imply from this sentence? Mrs. Garcia spends hours each night helping Javier with his homework.
   a. Mrs. Garcia is very patient
   b. Javier isn't a very good student.
   c. Mrs Garcia neglects her other children
   d. Javier is Mrs. Garcia's favorite son.

3. Infer the meaning of the missing word: Tim is quite athletic, though his brother is unfortunately, _____.
   a. fast
   b. tired
   c. uncoordinated
   d. artistic

4. The lights dimmed, the music began, and the people became silent. What can you reasonably infer from this sentence?
   a. It was time for bed.
   b. The movie was about to start.
   c. The store was closing.
   d. It was time for breakfast.

Inferences

Key Vocabulary

inference

Inferences

Use the clues in the images and match the conclusion by writing it in the box.

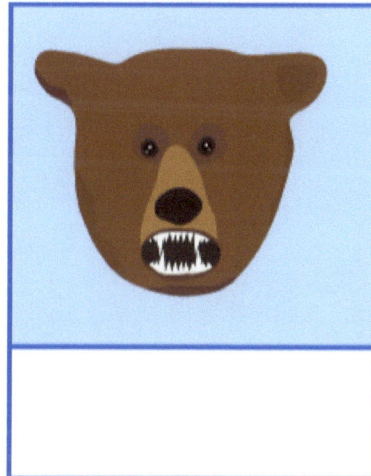

| This bear is angry. | The driver is probably OK. | Owen really likes this song. |

You've just made *inferences*. An **inference** is a conclusion made from what you *read* or *observe* combined with what you already *know*.

Read between the lines.

List the clues from the text and then draw a conclusion based on the clues.

Students, please put away your books and take out a pen and a blank piece of paper.

CLUES ●

Conclusion

Type to enter text

Readers should look for clues and use their own knowledge to help make an inference.

Complete the inference chart with the suggestions provided.

The theater lights dimmed and a message came on the screen asking patrons to turn cell phones off.

clues	prior knowledge	inference

the movie is about to begin	lights dim before a movie starts	theaters like people to be quiet
it is time to leave the movie theater	you need to buy your tickets	theaters want you to miss a call

Context Clues

Use context clues and prior knowledge to determine if the inferences are reasonable or not. Place a √ if the inference is reasonable and an X if it is not.

Tori was having a hard time falling asleep in the tent. She could hear the rustle of leaves and the snapping of twigs outside. A spooky owl hooted in the distance. "Did you hear that?" she asked her Dad.

☐ Tori is camping in the woods.

☐ Tori prefers hotel beds to tents.

☐ Tori is nervous.

☐ The forest is full of dangerous animals.

Use the clues to infer what is being discussed.

Under your inference, list the number of clues you needed to read to make your inference.

CLUES ●
I can't be left in the dark.
I've travelled to the moon.
People call me "Old Glory".
I have 13 horizontal stripes.

inference

CLUES ●
I eat grass.
I'm measured by "hands".
I can run at 30 mph.
I run in the Kentucky Derby.

inference

Imply vs. Infer

To **imply** is to put a suggestion *into* the message or text, while to **infer** is to to take a suggestion *out of the* message or text.

Hi Aunt Carmen. Thank for the yellow sweater that you gave me for my birthday. Although it went well with the pink shirt you gave me last year, I hope you don't mind that I exchanged it at the store.

Fernando **implies** that he doesn't really like the birthday gift that his aunt gave him!

Fernando, of course I don't mind that you exchanged the yellow sweater. I guess it was a bit old fashioned. I guess I don't have a good idea about what young people like.

Aunt Carmen has **inferred** that her nephew Fernando didn't really like the birthday gift she gave him!

Name_____

Inference Quiz

1. A read can sometimes use prior knowledge to make an inference? True or false.

2. What prior knowledge is most important to think about before going to a pool party?
    a. Pool parties can last a few hours.
    b. The water temperature may be cold at first.
    c. You will need to bring a swimsuit.
    d. Snacks will be served.

3. What can you infer about someone whispering to you?
    a. She is excited about what she is saying.
    b. She is unsure about what she is saying
    c. She is sad about what she is saying.
    d. She doesn't want anyone to hear what she is saying.

4. What can you infer about the weather if it is dark and cloudy in July.
    a. It is a good day to go to the beach.
    b. It may rain.
    c. It may snow.
    d. It will be sunny soon.

Context Clues

Key Vocabulary

context

synonym

antonym

root words

affix

Using Context Clues

What does the word jaunt mean?

A **context clue** can help a reader find the meaning of an unfamiliar word.

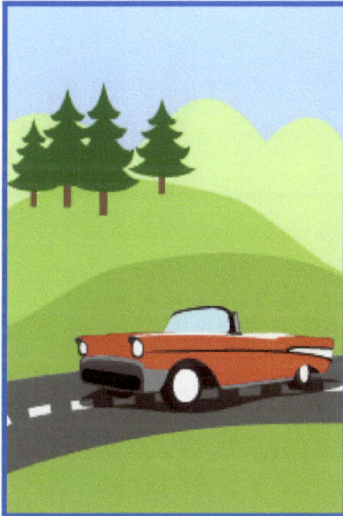

We took the car for a nice **jaunt** through the countryside.

- ○ gaze
- ○ picnic
- ○ trip
- ○ repair

Compare and Contrast

Synonyms and antonyms provide context clues. Select one of the word cards below to replace the highlighted word. Write the new word above or below the highlighted word.

Alison is **loquacious** ; she is chatty and always has something to say.

synonym

While Alison is loquacious, Anthony is much more **reticent** and quiet.

antonym

reserved	confusing	neat
tall	talkative	believable

_____

Context Clues in Text.

You can often find clues to the meaning of unknown words directly in the text. Complete the definitions below by referring to the text.

An archaeologist's main job is to study historical cultures, and one way they do this is by examining everyday objects from the past. These are called *artifacts*, and they provide many clues about the way people lived in the past. A good knowledge of geology (the study of the earth's structure) is essential in order to understand the significance of the artifacts and to date them properly.

archaeologists	
artifacts	
geology	

Root words and affixes as clues.

Root words and affixes can help define an unknown word. Use the word cards on the left to build the words.

bi

phobia

ology

photo

geo

cycle

	+		=	**?**
earth	+	study of	=	study of earth

	+		=	**?**
two	+	wheel	=	two wheels

	+		=	**?**
light	+	fear of	=	fear of light

Use what you know!

Use what you know about a sentence to find the meaning of an unknown word.

I took some medicine an hour ago to | alleviate | my headache. I feel a lot better now.

- ○ enhance
- ○ ignore
- ○ relieve
- ○ increase

_____

Using what you know about a sentence replace the highlighted words with one of the words below that mean the same thing. Write the new word above or below the highlighted word.

1 The | boisterous | fans were yelling loudly at the umpire and throwing popcorn.

2 The 22 photographers, 30 reporters, and 5 camera crews seemed | superfluous | for a bake sale.

3 I desperately need to do laundry because there is an | offensive | odor coming from the hamper.

calm	disgusting	pleasing
disorderly	lengthy	excessive

Name_____

Context Clues Quiz

1. "Although his mom wasn't very keen, he cajoled her into letting him go to the sleepover." The word *cajoled* means to promise. True or false?

2. Their vision was impaired by the heavy fog.
   1. unfamiliar
   2. obstructed
   3. damp
   4. improved

3. The cold and hungry solider needed a hearty meal.
   1. loving
   2. quick
   3. healthy
   4. filling

4. Our trepidation increased as the building gilled with more smoke.
   1. anxiety
   2. heart rate
   3. anger
   4. movement